WNBA

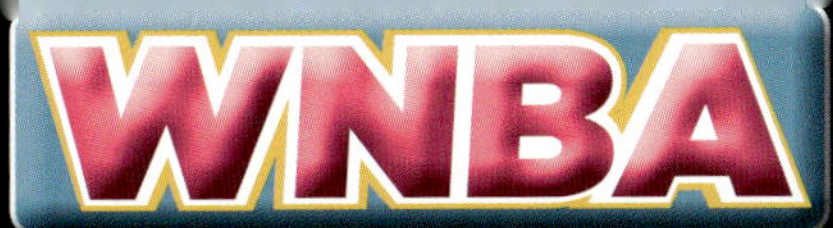

MINNESOTA LYNX

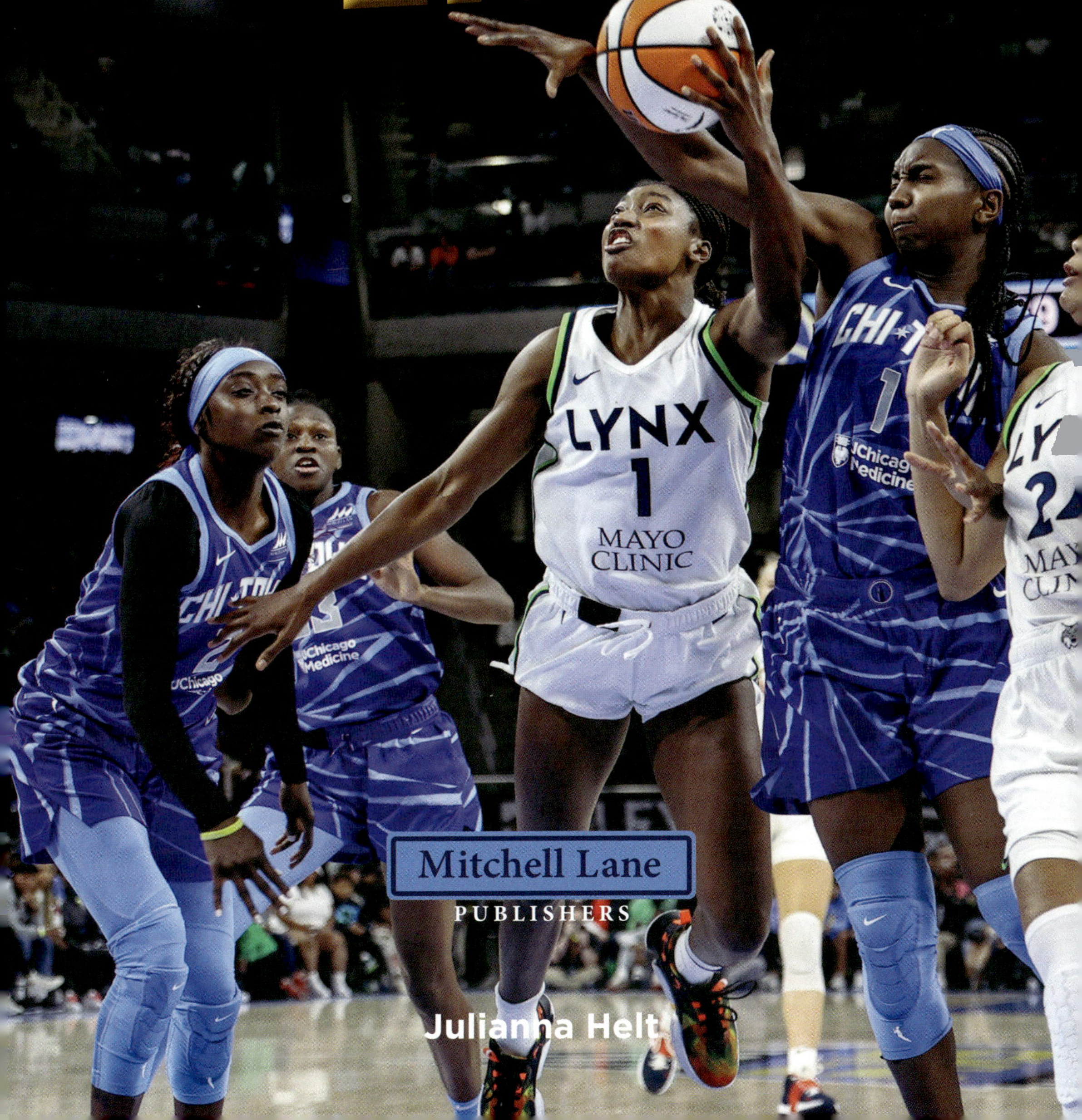

Mitchell Lane
PUBLISHERS

Julianna Helt

Mitchell Lane
PUBLISHERS

mitchelllanepub.com

2001 SW 31st Avenue
Hallandale, FL 33009

First Edition, 2026.
Author: Julianna Helt
Designer: Ed Morgan
Editor: Tammy Gagne

Series: WNBA
Title: Minnesota Lynx

Library bound ISBN: 979-8-89260-482-6
eBook ISBN: 979-8-89260-490-1

Photo credits: p. 11 Newscom.com; balance Alamy

CONTENTS

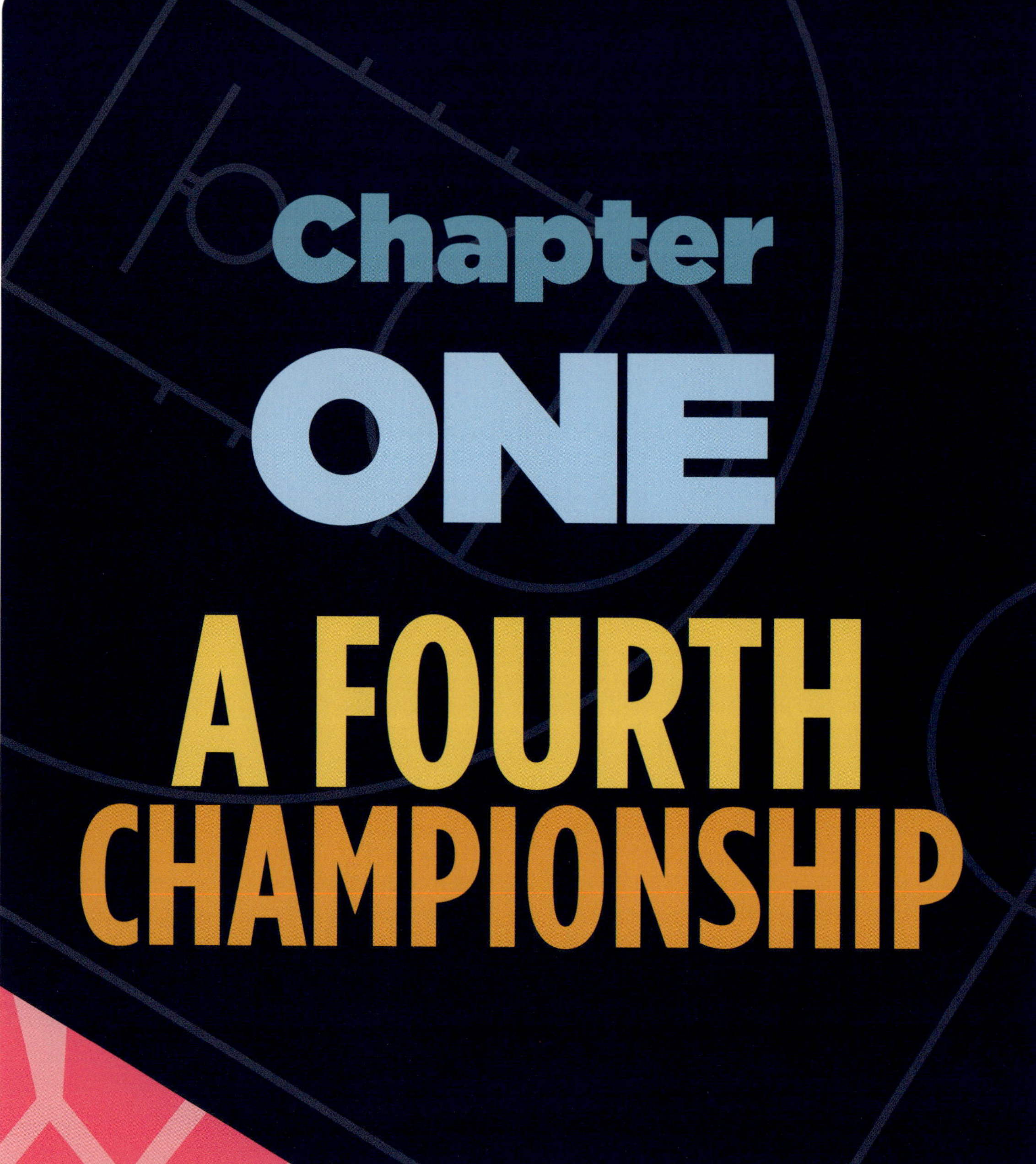

Chapter ONE
A FOURTH CHAMPIONSHIP

Minnesota Lynx forward Maya Moore after winning the 2017 WNBA Championship

In 2017, the Minnesota Lynx were out to prove themselves worthy of a championship title. The previous year ended with a devastating loss in the finals to the Los Angeles Sparks. The Lynx were determined not to let that happen again.

CHAPTER ONE

Sylvia Fowles shone in 2017 with one of her best seasons. She earned three **consecutive** Women's National Basketball Association (WNBA) Player of the Month awards between May and July. By August, the Lynx led the league in both points and **assists** per game.

The Lynx earned the number one seed heading into the playoffs. The Los Angeles Sparks earned the number two seed. Both teams swept their opponents in the semifinals. The stage was set for a repeat of the 2016 WNBA Finals.

The rivals split the first four games, each winning two games and forcing a fifth. The final game was played in front of a sold-out Minnesota crowd. The Lynx home court is Williams Arena, nicknamed the Barn for its pitched roof. Los Angeles put up a tough fight. The lead went back and forth between the teams until the clock ran out with Minnesota on top. The final score was 85–76. The Lynx won their fourth championship in seven years.

A Fourth Championship

FAST FACT

Sylvia Fowles is the WNBA's career leader in rebounds, with 3,712.

CHAPTER ONE

Point guard Lindsay Whalen told the *SunStar* website, "I think every time you do this it gets a little more special, because it gets a little harder. And more meaningful because you know it's not easy." But the Lynx sure made it look easy. Whalen had 17 points and 18 assists in the game.

Sylvia Fowles also scored 17 points and racked up 20 **rebounds**. She was named the Finals MVP. With 18 points and 10 rebounds, Maya Moore also heavily contributed to the win. She responded to her fourth championship by telling ESPN. "I don't know if you are going to get a more deep, committed, selfless group than we have here."

A Fourth Championship

Lindsay Whalen drives to the basket.

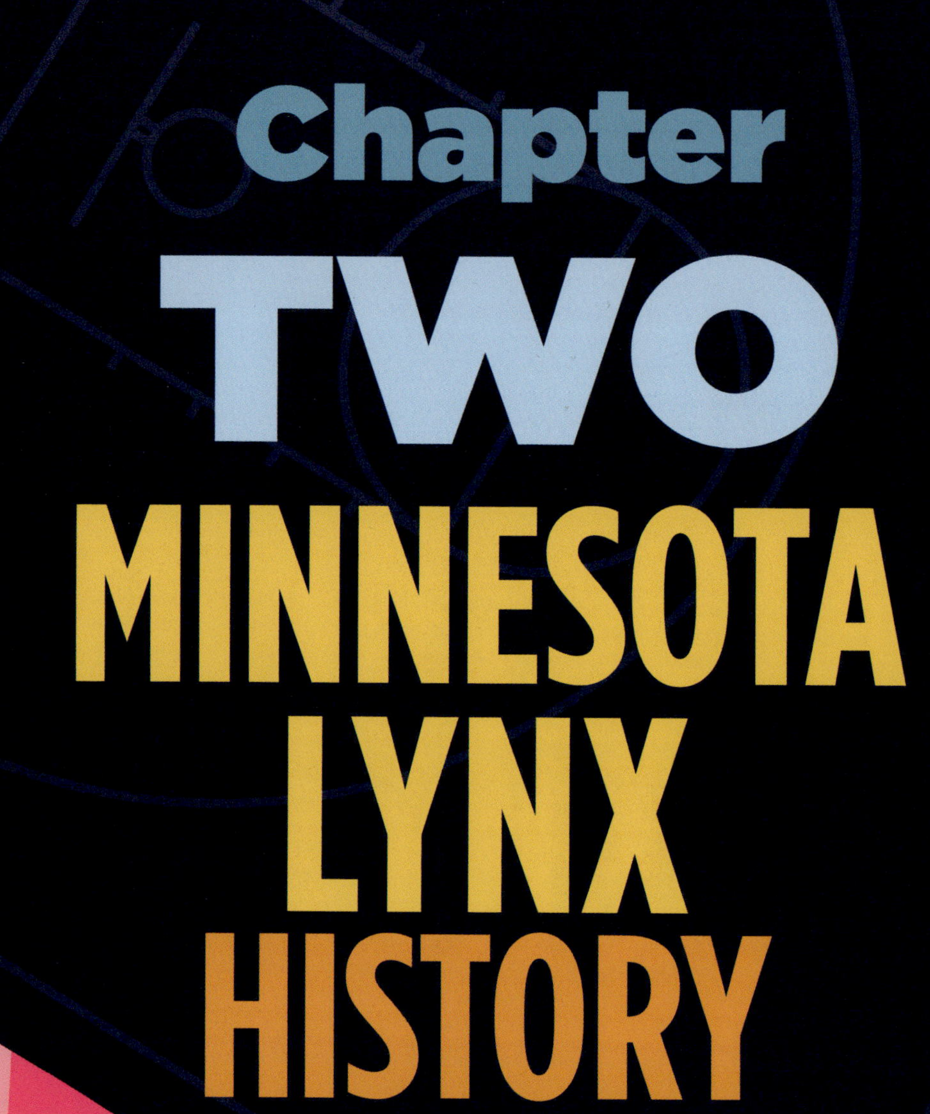

Chapter TWO MINNESOTA LYNX HISTORY

Minnesota Lynx logo 1999–2010

The Minnesota Lynx joined the WNBA as an **expansion team** in 1999. The team had a combined 47–76 record for its first four seasons. The Lynx missed out on the playoffs each year.

CHAPTER TWO

In 2003, the Lynx finished with a then franchise-best 18–16 record. They advanced to the WNBA playoffs for the first time. They won their first-ever playoff game with a dramatic 21-point **comeback** in game one. But they ultimately lost the series.

The team also did well in 2004, making it to the Western Conference semifinals again. The Lynx began to struggle after that. They endured six consecutive losing seasons.

The Lynx began to turn things around in the 2010s. They advanced to the playoffs for nine straight seasons. This included six trips to the WNBA Finals with four championship wins.

Minnesota Lynx History

Minnesota Lynx players (left to right) Maya Moore, Seimone Augustus, Taj McWilliams-Franklin, and Lindsay Whalen

FAST FACT

The Lynx were the only professional sports team to win four championships in the 2010s.

CHAPTER TWO

The team's success started with the 2011 WNBA Draft. The Lynx selected Maya Moore of the University of Connecticut at the yearly event. In the 2011 season, Minnesota had a league-best record, 27–7. They went on to sweep the Atlanta Dream in the finals, winning their first championship.

The team was invited to the White House after the 2011 win. President Barack Obama said in his welcome speech, "The team had the best record in the league. They made their home games the hottest ticket in town."

The Lynx continued their success by defeating the Atlanta Dream again in 2013 for their second title in three years. The Lynx defeated the Indiana Fever in game five of the finals in 2015, earning Minnesota its third championship that year. The Lynx won their fourth title in 2017, defeating the Los Angeles Sparks. With their fourth championship win, the Minnesota Lynx cemented their place in WNBA history.

Minnesota Lynx History

President Barack Obama honors the 2015 WNBA champion, the Minnesota Lynx.

Chapter THREE

HEAD COACH CHERYL REEVE

Coach Cheryl Reeve instructs her team.

Cheryl Reeve became the Lynx's head coach in 2010. She had been the assistant coach for the Detroit Shock, a team that moved to Oklahoma before settling in Texas as the Dallas Wings. Reeve won two championships in Detroit. With the Lynx, Reeve has led the team to six finals and all four of their championships.

CHAPTER THREE

Cheryl Reeve has spoken about her coaching **philosophy**. She told the *Winona Daily News*, "The most powerful thing we do is show boys strong powerful women at a young age. When they grow up, become leaders, their mindset is different."

The Lynx ended the 2010 season with a 13–21 record. Reeve helped turn the team around the next season. Minnesota ended its regular season with a record of 27–7 in 2011. The Lynx also won the championship title that year. Reeve was named WNBA Coach of the Year at the end of 2011. She went on to lead the team to championship titles in 2013 and 2015.

Head Coach Cheryl Reeve

Lynx guard Courtney Williams during a game

CHAPTER THREE

Reeve led the Lynx to a league-best 28–6 record in 2016. She was again named Coach of the Year. The following year, the Lynx won their fourth championship.

In 2020, Reeve had the highest winning percentage in both the regular season and the postseason in league history. She was also named Coach of the Year in 2020, becoming the third coach in league history to win the award three times.

Lindsay Whalen told the *Winona Daily News*, "There is such a connection. We all know she's the coach. She is in charge, she built this thing. But we're all in this together."

Head Coach Cheryl Reeve

FAST FACT

In 2021, Cheryl Reeve coached the U.S. Women's National Team to a gold medal at the Tokyo Olympics.

Chapter FOUR

SUPERSTAR LYNX PLAYERS

Lynx forward Napheesa Collier goes for a two pointer.

Napheesa Collier joined the Lynx in 2019. She was selected sixth in the first round of the WNBA Draft. Collier played college basketball at the University of Connecticut. Known to many by her nickname *Phee*, she exploded in her first year with the Lynx, earning the **Rookie** of the Year award.

CHAPTER FOUR

Coach Cheryl Reeve spoke about Collier's rookie season in a press conference. She said the **consistency** that Collier demonstrates is rarely seen in a player's first year. "[S]imply put, we were a better team with her on the court," Reeve said. Collier became the fourth Lynx player to earn Rookie of the Year. She was also the fourth player in WNBA history to finish a season with at least 400 points.

Collier continued to impress her coach, teammates, and fans after her rookie season. She is a four-time WNBA All-Star. She moved into a leadership role in the 2023 season, being named captain. Reeve told reporters, "Sometimes you have superstars that don't have time for other people. Phee is just the opposite of that."

Superstar Lynx Players

Seimone Augustus

FAST FACT

Many Lynx players have represented the United States at the Olympics. The list includes Seimone Augustus, Sylvia Fowles, Maya Moore, and Lindsay Whalen.

CHAPTER FOUR

Kayla McBride is another Lynx superstar. She was drafted third overall by the San Antonio Stars in 2014. The Stars later became the Las Vegas Aces. McBride was named to the All-Star team three times before being traded to Minnesota in 2021.

She was selected to the All-Star team for the fourth time as a member of the Lynx in 2024. She was fourth in the league for three pointers. She made 64 of her 148 attempts. McBride has helped the Lynx to its best overall record since 2017.

Some basketball fans may worry that the Lynx **dynasty** ended with their championship in 2017. They came close to a fifth title in 2024, losing to the New York Liberty in game five of the finals. But with Cheryl Reeve at the helm and plenty of star power, other fans insist that the Minnesota Lynx dynasty is still very much alive.

Superstar Lynx Players

Lynx guard Kayla McBride secures the ball.

GLOSSARY

assists
Passes made to teammates, which lead to scored points

comeback
A return to a former position

consecutive
Directly following another instance

consistency
The ability to perform dependably regardless of the opponent or situation

dynasty
A team or other group with a long history of success

expansion team
A new team that is added to an existing league

philosophy
An individual's basic belief system or approach to a topic

point guard
A basketball player who brings the ball up the court and sets up offensive plays

rebounds
Caught basketballs after missed shots

rookie
An athlete playing her first season as a member of a professional sports team

SLAM DUNK WNBA TRIVIA

- Minnesota's mascot is a lynx named Prowl.
- The Minnesota Lynx play their home games at the Target Center in Minneapolis. They share the arena with the Minnesota Timberwolves, a National Basketball Association (NBA) team.
- The Lynx's team colors are blue, green, and gray.
- The team's sponsor is the Mayo Clinic, which is in Rochester, Minnesota.
- Maya Moore was named *Sports Illustrated*'s Performer of the Year after winning her fourth WNBA Championship 2017.
- The points leader for the Lynx is Seimone Augustus. She scored 5,881 points in her career, placing her among the top ten points leaders for the entire WNBA.

FIND OUT MORE

IN PRINT

Crooks-Johnson, Jenny. *Dallas Wings*. Mitchell Lane Publishers, 2026.

Davidson, B. Keith. *WNBA*. Crabtree Publishing, 2022.

O'Neal, Ciara. *The WNBA Finals*. Apex, 2023.

ON THE INTERNET

Minnesota Lynx.
https://lynx.wnba.com.

"Minnesota Lynx," *ESPN*, n.d.
www.espn.com/wnba/team/_/name/min/minnesota-lynx.

"Minnesota Lynx," *FOX Sports*, n.d.
www.foxsports.com/wnba/minnesota-lynx-team.

INDEX

About the Author

Julianna Helt is a children's-librarian-turned-author. She enjoys researching and writing about all sorts of topics, including women in sports. Her favorite WNBA player is Caitlin Clark. When Julianna isn't writing, she enjoys reading and solving puzzles. She lives with her family in Pittsburgh, Pennsylvania.